20
38
968

DISCARD
RETIRÉ

NUMBER 45

THE ENGLISH
EXPERIENCE

ITS RECORD IN EARLY PRINTED BOOKS
PUBLISHED IN FACSIMILE

EDWARD PELLHAM

GODS POWER
AND PROVIDENCE

LONDON 1631

DA CAPO PRESS
THEATRVM ORBIS TERRARVM LTD.
AMSTERDAM 1968 NEW YORK

The publishers acknowledge their gratitude
to the Trustees of the Bodleian Library, Oxford,
for their permission to reproduce
the Library's copy.

S.T.C.No.19566

Collation: $A-E^4, F^2$.

Published in 1968 by
Theatrum Orbis Terrarum Ltd.,
O.Z. Voorburgwal 85, Amsterdam
&
Da Capo Press
- a division of Plenum Publishing Corporation -
227 West 17th Street, New York. 10011
Library of Congress Catalog Card Number:

68 – 54656

Printed in The Netherlands

Gods Power and Providence:

Shewed,

IN THE MIRACV-
lous Preservation and Deliverance
of eight Englishmen, left by mischance
in *Green-land* Anno 1630. nine moneths
and twelve dayes.

With a true Relation *of all their miseries,*
their shifts and hardship they were put to,
their food, *&c.* such as neither *Heathen*
nor *Christian* men ever before endured.

With a Description of the chiefe Places *and*
Rarities of that barren and cold Countrey.

Faithfully reported by EDVVARD PELLHAM,
one of the eight men aforesaid.

As also with a Map of G R E E N-L A N D.

---

*They that goe downe into the Sea in ships ; that doe businesse
in great waters :*
These see the workes of the Lord, and his wonders in the deepe.
PSAL. 107.23,24.

LONDON,
Printed by R. Y. for IOHN PARTRIDGE, and are
to be sold at the Signe of the *Sunne* in
Pauls Church-yard. 1631.

69-1541

To the right VVor-

ſhipfull Sir HVGH HAMMERSLY Knight, Alderman of the Citie of London, Governour of the Worſhipfull Company of *the Muſcovia Merchants* :

And to the VVorſhipfull, Mr Alderman Freeman, Captaine William Goodler: And to all the reſt of the Worſhipfull Aſſiſtants and Adventurers in the ſaid famous *Company.* Edward Pellham *dedicateth both this and his future Labours.*

Right Worſhipfull and moſt famous Merchants:

He hard adventure my poore ſelfe and fellowes underwent in your Worſhips ſervice, is a great deale pleaſanter for others to reade, than it was for us to endure. How ever hard, wee have now endured it; and if ever after-

ages

ages shall speake of it, (as the world still doth of the *Dutch-mens* hard Winter in *nova Zembla* :) thus much of the Voyage shall redound to your honours, that it was done by your Servants. This may also returne to our Countreys good; That if the first inhabiting of a Countrey by a Princes Subiects (which is the King of *Spaines* best title to his *Indyes*) doth take possession of it for their *Soveraigne* : Then is *Green-land* by a second right taken *livery* and *Seisin* of, for his *Majesties* use; his Subiects being the first that ever did (and I beleeve the last that ever will) inhabite there. Many a rich returne may your Worships in generall, and the brave Adventurers in particular receive from this and all other places: and may your Servants be ever hereafter, warned to take heede by our harmes. God send your Worships long life, and much honour, and sufficient wealth, to maintaine both. This is the hearty prayer of your Worships poore servant

Edward Pellham.

TO

To the Reader.

Ourteous Reader : That God may have the onely glory of this our deliverance, give mee leave to looke backe unto that voyage, which the Dutch-men *made into* Nova Zembla, *in the yeare* 1596. *In which place, they having beene (like our selves) overtaken with the Winter, were there forced to stay it out as wee were. Which being an Action so famous all the world over, encouraged mee both to publish this of ours, as also now to draw out some comparisons with them: that so our deliverance, and Gods glory may appeare both the more gracious and the greater.*

This Nova Zembla *stands in the Degree* 76. *North latitude : our wintering place is in* 77. *Degrees and* 40. *Minutes, that is, almost two Degrees neerer the North* Pole *than they were; and so much therefore the colder. The* Dutch *were furnished with all things necessary both for* life and health; *had no want of any thing:* Bread, Beere, *and* Wine, *they had good, and good store.* Victuals *they had Gods plenty; and Apparell both for present clothing; and for shift too : and all this they brought with them in their Ship. We (God knowes)*

wanted

To the Reader.

wanted all these. Bread, Beere, *and* Wine *we had none.
As for meate, our greatest and chiefest feeding was the*
Whale Frittars, *and those mouldie too ; the loathsomest
meate in the world. For our* Venison *, 'twas hard to
finde, but a great deale harder to get : and for our third
sort of provision the* Beares, *'twas a measuring cast
which should be eaten first,* Wee *or the* Beares, *when we
first saw one another : and we perceived by them, that
they had as good hopes to devoure us, as wee to kill them.
The* Dutch kill'd *Beares*, *'tis true : but it was for their
skinnes, not for their flesh. The* Dutch *had a* Surgeon
in their Companie; wee none but the great Physician *to
take care and cure of us. They had the benefite of* Ba-
thing *and* Purging : *wee of neither. They had their
Ship at hand to be friend them ; wee had here perished,
had not other Ships fetcht us off. They had* Card *and*
Compasse, *wee no direction.*

If the Dutch *complained therefore of the extremity
of the cold, (as well they might) and that when in building their house, they (as* Carpenters *use to doe) put the
iron nayles into their mouthes, they there froze, and
stucke so fast, that they brought off the skinne and forced
blood : how cold, thinke you, were we, that were faine to
maintaine two fires to keepe our very morter from freezing. The* Dutch *complain'd, that their walls were frozen two inches thicke on the inside for all their fire : and
if ours were not so, 'twas our paines and industry at first
in building. The* Dutch-mens *clothes froze upon
their backes, and their shooes were like hornes upon their
feete : but that was their owne ignorance; for they had
Sea-coles enough with them, if they had knowne how to
use them. If their drinke and Sacke were so hard fre-*
zen

To the Reader.

zen into lumps of yce, that they were faine to cut it out;
how much harder was it for us, that were forced to make
hot irons our best toasts to warme the snow withall, for
our mornings draughts? They used heated stones and
billets to their feete and bodies, to warme them: which,
though an hard shift, yet was it better than we had any.

Lay now all these together, the distance of place, wee
being many miles more into the cold than they: the
want both of meate and clothes; and that the house wee
lived in, we had but three dayes respite to build for nine
moneths to come; and then may the world see, that the
Dutch had the better provisions, and wee the abler
bodies. If therefore the Dutch-mens deliverance
were worthily accounted a wonder, ours can amount to
little lesse than a miracle. The greater therefore our
deliverance, the greater must be Gods glory. And that's
the Authors purpose in publishing of it. God keepe
the Readers from the like dangers. So
prayes he that endured what
he here writes of

Edw. Pellham.

The

The names of the Men thus staying in GREEN-LAND, for nine moneths and twelve dayes

VV*Illiam Fakely*, Gunner. *Edward Pellham*, Gunners mate, the Author of this Relation. *Iohn Wise*, and *Robert Goodfellow*, Sea-men. *Thomas Ayers*, Whale-cutter. *Henry Bett*, Cooper. *Iohn Dawes*, and *Richard Kellet*, Land-men.

GODS

Gods Power and Providence in the preservation of eight Men in GREEN-LAND, nine Moneths and twelve Dayes.

But wee had the sentence of death in our selves, that wee should not trust in our selves, but in God which raiseth the dead.
Who delivered us from so great a death, and doth deliver: in whom wee trust that hee will yet deliver us.
2. Cor. 1. ver. 9, 10.

REENLAND is a Country very farre Northward, situated in 77. degrees, and 40. minutes, that is, within 12. degrees and 20. minutes of the very North Pole it selfe. The Land is wonderfull mountainous, the Mountaines all the year long full of yce and snow: the Plaines in part bare in Sum-

B   mer

mer time. There growes neither tree nor hearbe in
it, except *Scurvygraffe* and *Sorrell*. The Sea is as
barren as the Land , affording no fish but Whales,
Sea-horfes,Seales,& another fmall fish.And hither
there is a yearely Fleet of English fent. Wee eight
men therefore being employed in the fervice of the
Right Worfhipfull Company of *Mufcowie* Merchants , in the good fhip called the *Salutation* of
London, were bound for this *Greenland* aforefaid,to
make a voyage upon *Whales* or *Sea-horfe*, for the advantage of the Merchants , and the good of the
Common-wealth. Wee fet fayle from *London* the
firft day of *May*, 1630. and having a faire gale,wee
quickly left the fertile bankes of *Englands* pleafant
fhoares behinde us. After which,fetting our comely
fayles to this fuppofed profperous gale,and ranging
through the boyfterous billowes of the rugged
Seas , by the helpe and gracious affiftance of Almighty God,wee fafely arrived at our defired Port,
in*Greenland*,the eleventh of *Iune* following.Wher-
upon having moored our fhips , and carryed our
caske athoare , wee , with all expedition , fell to the
fitting up of our Shallops, with all things neceffarie
for our intended voyage. Wee were in companie
three Ships; all which were then appointed by the
order of our Captaine, *Captaine William Goodler*, to
ftay at the *Foreland*, untill the fifteenth of *Iuly*; with
refolution, that if we could not by that time make a
voyage according to our expectation, then, to fend
one fhip to the Eaftward, unto a fifhing place fome
fourefcore leagues from thence; whither at the lat-
ter end of the yeare,the Whales ufe more frequently

ly to resort. A second of the three ships was designed for *Green-harbour*,(a place some fifteene leagues distant to the *Southward*) there to trie her skill and fortune, if it were possible there to make a voyage. The third ship (which was the same wherein wee were) was appointed to stay at the *Fore-land*, untill the twentieth of *August*. But the Captaine having made a great voyage at *Bell Sownd*, dispatches a Shallop towards our ship, with a command unto us to come to him at *Bell Sownd* aforesaid : his purpose being,both to have us take in some of his *Trane Oyle*, as also by joyning our forces together, to make the Fleete so much the stronger for the defence of the Merchants goods homeward bound, the *Dunkirkers* being very strong and rife at sea in those dayes. Upon the eighth day of *August* (thereupon) leaving the *Foreland*, wee directed our course to the *Southward*, towards *Green-harbour*,there to take in twenty of our men, which had out of our ships company beene sent into the lesser ship, for the furtherance of her voyage.

But the winde being now contrary,our ship could no way *lye our course*.The fifteenth day,being calme and cleare, and our ship now in the *Offing*, some foure leagues from *Blacke-point*,and about five from the *Maydens pappes* (which is a place famous, both for very good, and for great store of *Venison*,) our Master sent us eight men here named, altogether in a shallop for the hunting and killing of some Venison, for the ships provision. Wee thus leaving the ship, and having taken a brace of dogs along with us, and furnisht our selves with a snap-hance, two

lances, and a tinder-boxe; wee directed our courfe
towards the shoare, where in foure houres wee arrived, the weather being at that time faire and
cleare, and every way feafonable for the perfor-
mance of our prefent intentions. That day we laid
fourteene tall and nimble Deere along; and being
very weary and throughly tyred (firft with rowing,
and now with hunting)wee fell to eate fuch victuals
as wee had brought along; agreeing to take our reft
for that night, and the next day to make an end of
our hunting, and fo fairely to returne to our fhip a-
gaine. But the next day, as it pleafed God, the
weather falling out fomething thicke,and much yce
in the *Offing* betwixt the fhoare and the fhip (by
reafon of a Southerly winde driving alongft the
coaft) our fhip was forced fo farre to *ftand off* into
the Sea, to be cleare of the yce, that wee had quite
loft the fight of her : neither could wee affure our
felves, whether fhee were inclofed in the drift yce,
or not : and the weather ftill growing thicker and
thicker,we thought it our beft courfe to hunt alongft
the fhoare, and fo to goe for *Greene-harbour*,there to
ftay aboard the fhip with the reft of our men, vntill
our own fhip fhould come into the Port.

Coafting thus along towards *Greene-harbour*,wee
kill'd eight Deere more; and fo at laft having well
loaden our Shallop with Venifon, wee ftill kept on
our courfe towards *Green-harbour* : where arriving
upon the feventeenth day, wee found (to our great
wonderment)that the fhip was departed thence, together with our twenty men aforefaid. That which
increafed our admiration was, for that wee knew
                                                    they

they had not victuals sufficient aboard, to serve them (by *proportion*) homewards bownd: which made vs againe to wonder what should be the reason of their so sudden departure.

Perceiving our selves hus frustrated of our expectation, and having now but bare three dayes(according to appointment) to the uttermost expiration of our limited time for our departure out of the Country; we thought it our best course to make all possible speed to get to *Bell Sownd*, unto our Captaine ; fearing that a little delay might bring a great deale of danger. For the lightening therefore of our Shallop, that she might make the better way through the waters, wee heaved our Venison overboard, and cast it all into the Sea. Having thus forsaken *Green-harbour*, with a longing desire to recover *Bell Sownd* (from thence distant some sixteene leagues to the *Southward*) that night wee got halfe way about the point of the *Nesse*, or point of land, called *Low-Nesse*: But the darknesse or mistie fogge increasing so fast upon us, that it was impossible for us to get further, even there betweene two rocks we coved from the seventeenth day at night, untill the eighteenth day at noone. At which time the weather being somewhat clearer (though very thicke still) wee left the *Nesse* behinde us, still desirous to recover *Bell Sownd*: but having never a *Compasse* to direct our course by, nor any of our company that was *Pilot* sufficient to know the land when he saw it, we were faine to grabble in the darke (as it were) like a blinde man for his way, and so over-shot *Bell point* at least tenne leagues to the *Southward*, to-

wards

wards *Horne Sownd.*

Some of us in the meane time knowing that it was impoſſible to bee ſo long a rowing and ſayling of eight leagues (for wee did both row and ſayle) made enquirie, *How the Harbour lay in?* whereunto there was a ready anſwer made, *That it lay Eaſt in.* Taking the matter therefore into our better conſideration, ſome of us judged, that it could not poſſibly be further to the *Southward* (our reaſon being, our obſervation of the lands *rounding away* and *trenting* towards the *Eaſtward*) and reſolved thereupon to row no further on that Courſe, for the finding of *Bell Sownd.* And though wee were againe perſwaded by *William Fakely* our Gunner, (a proper Sea-man, though no skilfull Mariner, who had been in the Country five or ſixe times before; which none of our Sea-men had beene) that it was further to the *Southwards:* yet we, truſting better to our own reaſons than unto his perſwaſions, againe returned towards the *Northward:* which was our beſt and directeſt Courſe indeed, for the finding of *Bell Sownd.* Steering of which Courſe, wee were now come within two miles of *Bell Point,* & the weather being faire and cleare, wee preſently deſcryed the tops of the loftie mountaines. *William Fakely* thereupon looking about him, preſently cries out unto us, *That wee were all this while upon a wrong Courſe:* upon hearing of which words, ſome of our companie (yea the moſt) were perſwaded, to *wend* about the Boates head the ſecond time, unto the *Southwards:* which one action was the maine and onely cauſe of our too late repentance, though for mine owne

owne part (as it is well knowne) I never gave consent unto their counsell.

And thus upon the fatall twentieth day of *August*,
(which was the utmoſt day of our limited time for
ſtaying in the Country) wee againe returned the
quite contrary way, namely to the *Southward*. Thus
utterly uncertaine when and where to finde the
Sownd; a thouſand ſadde imaginations overtooke
our perplexed minds, all of us aſſuredly knowing,
that a million of miſeries would of neceſſitie enſue,
if wee found not the ſhips, whereby to ſave our paſ-
ſage. In this diſtracted time of our thoughts, wee
were now againe the ſecond time runne as farre to
the *Southward* as at the firſt : and finding by all reaſon thereupon, how that there was no likelihood at
all of finding any ſuch place further to the *Southward*, we *wended* the Shallop the ſecond time unto
the *Northward*. *William Fakely* hereupon, being
unwilling to condeſcend unto our agreement, ſtill
perſwaded us, that *That could not poſſibly bee our
Courſe* : but we not truſting any longer unto his un-
skilfull perſwaſions, (though all in him was out of
good will, and ſtrong conceit of his being in the
rights)bent our Courſe to the *Northward*; and hee
not conſenting to ſteere any longer, I tooke the
Oare out of his hand to ſteere the Boate withall.
The weather all this while continued faire and
cleare, and it pleaſed God at the very inſtant time,
to ſend the winde *Eaſterly* : which advantage wee
thankfully apprehending, preſently ſet ſayle. The
winde increaſed freſh and large, and our Shallop
ſwiftly running, we arrived the one and twentieth
day

day at *Bell point*, where wee found the winde right
out of the *Sownd* at *Eaſt Northeaſt* ſo fiercely blow-
ing, that we could not poſſibly row to *Wind-wards*;
but being forced to take in our ſayle, we were faine
to betake our ſelves unto our Oares : by helpe of
which wee recovered ſome two miles within the
ſhoare, where we were conſtrained for that time to
Cove, or elſe to drive to *Lee-wards*.

Thus finding this to be the very place we had all
this while ſought for,(he now alſo agreeing there-
unto)we forthwith ſought out and found an harbor
for our *Shallop* : and having brought *her* thereinto,
two of our men were preſently diſpatched over
land unto the *Tent* at *Bell Sownd*, to ſee if the Ships
were ſtill there; of which, by reaſon of the times
being expired, and the opportunitie of the preſent
faire winde,wee were much afraid. The *Tent* being
diſtant ten miles at the leaſt from our Shallop, our
men at their comming thither finding the ſhips to
be departed out of the Roade, and not being certaine, whether or not they might be at *Bottle Cove*,
(three leagues diſtant on the other ſide of the *Sownd*)
riding there under the *Loome* of the land; againe returne unto us with this ſadde newes. The ſtorme of
winde hitherto continuing, about mid-night fell
ſtarke calme : whereupon we,unwilling to loſe our
firſt opportunity,departed towards *Bottle Cove*; betwixt hope and feare of finding the ſhips there:
whither comming the two & twentieth,and finding
the ſhips departed, we, having neither *Pilot*, *Plat*,
nor *Compaſſe* for our directors to the *Eaſtward*,
found our ſelves (God he knoweth) to have little
hope

hope of any delivery out of that apparent danger.
Our feares increafed upon us, even whil'ft we con-
fulted whether it were fafeft for us either to goe or
ftay. If goe, then thought wee upon the dangers in
fayling, by reafon of the much yce in the way; as
alfo of the difficultie in finding the place, when wee
fhould come thereabouts. If we refolved ftill to remaine at *Bell Sownd*, then wee thought that no other
thing could be looked for, but a miferable and a pining death, feeing there appeared no poffibility of
inhabiting there, or to endure fo long, fo darkfome,
and fo bitter a winter.

And thus were our thoughts at that time diftra-
cted, thus were our feares increafed; nor were they
caufeleffe feares altogether. Well, wee knew that
neither *Chriftian* or *Heathen* people, had ever before
inhabited thofe defolate and untemperate *Clymates*.
This alfo, to increafe our feares, had wee certainly
heard; how that the *Merchants* having in former
times much defired, and that with proffer of great
rewards for the hazarding of their lives, and of fuf-
ficient furniture and provifion of all things that
might bee thought neceffary for fuch an undertaking, to any that would adventure to winter in thofe
parts; could never yet finde any fo hardy, as to ex-
pofe their lives unto fo hazardous an undertaking:
yea notwithftanding thefe proffers had beene made
both unto Mariners of good experience, and of
noble refolutions, and alfo unto divers other bold
fpirits; yet had the action of wintering in thofe
parts, never by any beene hitherto undertaken. This
alfo had we heard, how that the company of *Muf-*
covie

covie Merchants, having once procured the reprive of some malefactors, that had here at home beene convicted by Law for some haynous crimes committed; and that both with promise of pardon for their faults, and with addition of rewards also, if so be they would undertake to remaine in *Green-land* but one whole yeare, and that every way provided for too, both of Clothes, Victuals, and all things else, that might any way be needfull for their preservation: These poore wretches hearing of this large proffer, & fearing present execution at home, resolved to make tryall of the adventure. The time of yeare being come, and the ships ready to depart, these condemned creatures are imbarked, who after a certaine space there arriving, and taking a view of the desolatenesse of the place; they conceived such a horrour and inward feare in their hearts, as that they resolved rather to returne for *England* to make satisfaction with their lives for their former faults committed, than there to remaine, though with assured hope of gaining their pardon: Insomuch as the time of the yeare being come, that the ships were to depart from these barren shoares, they made knowne their full intent unto the Captaine: who being a pittifull and a mercifull Gentleman, would not by force constraine them to stay in that place, which was so contrary to their minds; but having made his voyage by the time expired; hee againe imbarked and brought them over with him into *England*, where, through the intercession and meanes of the Worshipfull Companie of *Muscovie* Merchants, they escaped

that

that death, which they had before beene condemned unto. The remembrance of these two former stories, as also of a third (more terrible than both the former, for that it was likely to be our own case) more miserably now affrighted us: and that was the lamentable and unmanly ends of nine good and able men, left in the same place heretofore by the selfe same Master that now left us behinde: who all dyed miserably upon the place, being cruelly disfigured after their deaths by the savage Beares and hungry Foxes, which are not onely the civilest, but also the onely inhabitants of that comfortlesse Countrey: the lamentable ends and miscarriage of which men, had beene enough indeed to have daunted the spirits of the most noble resolution.

All these fearefull examples presenting themselves before our eyes, at this place of *Bottle Cove* aforesaid, made us, like amazed men, to stand looking one upon another, all of us, as it were, beholding in the present, the future calamities both of himselfe and of his fellowes. And thus, like men already metamorphosed into the yce of the Country, and already past both our sense and reason; stood wee with the eyes of pittie beholding one another.

Nor was it other mens examples and miscarriages and feares alone, that made us amazed, but it was the consideration of our want of all necessary provision for the life of man, that already strooke us to the heart: For we were not only unprovided, both of clothes to keepe us warme, and of foode to prevent the wrath of cruell famine: but vtterly destitute also wee were of a sufficient house, wherein to

shrowd

shrowd and shelter our selves from the chilling cold. Thus for a space standing all mute and silent, weighing with our selves the miserie wee were already fallen into, and knowing delay in these extremities to be the mother of all dangers, we began to conceive hope, even out of the depth of despaire. Rowsing up our benummed senses therefore, wee now lay out heads and counsels together, to bethinke our selves of the likeliest course for our preservation in that place; seeing that all hopes of gaining our passage into *England*, were then quite frustrate. Shaking off therefore all childish and effeminate feares, it pleased God to give us hearts like men, to arme our selves with a resolution to doe our best for the resisting of that monster of Desperation. An agreement thereupon by a generall consent of the whole Companie we then entred into, to take the opportunity of the next faire weather, and goe for *Green-harbour*, to hunt and kill Venison for part of our winter provision.

Having thus agreed amongst our selves, the five and twentieth day of *August*, the weather and wind being both faire, wee direct our course towards *Green-harbour*, some sixteene leagues (as I before told you) distant from *Bell Sownd*: and the winde being fresh and faire, within the space of twelve houres we there arrived. Upon which place being now landed, the first thing we did, was to make us a Tent with the sayle of our Shallop, pitcht up and spread upon our Oares; a sorry one (God knowes) though it were, yet under it we resolved to rest our selves that night, to refresh our bodies with such food

food as wee there had , and the next day to returne
againe unto our hunting. The weather that night
proving faire and cleare , wee made our ſleepe the
ſhorter : (and alas what men could ſleepe in ſuch an
extremitie !) and fitting our ſelves and Shallop the
beſt we might, to *Coles Parke* we went, a place ſome
two leagues diſtant from us, and well knowne unto
Thomas Ayers, that was one of our Companie,to be
well ſtored with Veniſon. Comming a-ſhoare at
which place, though we found not ſo many Deere
as we indeed expected,yet ſeven we killed the ſame
day,and foure Beareſto boote; which wee alſo intended to eate.

But the weather beginning now to overcaſt , and
not likely to continue good for hunting ; wee that
night returned againe unto *Green-harbour* : where
making us a Tent of our *Sayle* and *Oares*(as is before
deſcribed) we fell to eate of ſuch meate as God had
ſent us , and betooke our ſelves to our reſt upon it.
Having reſted our ſelves a while , and now finding
the weather to cleare up, we broke off our ſleepe for
that time, fitting our ſelves and two dogges againe
to goe a hunting; leaving *William Fakely* and *Iohn
Dawes* behinde us in the Tent at *Green-harbour* , as
our Cookes(for the time)to dreſſe ſome meate that
wee had, for our refreſhment at our returne.

Departing thus from the Tent , wee rowed towards *Coles Parke*;in the way whither,upon the ſide
of a hill, by the Sea ſide , wee eſpyed ſeven Deere
feeding , whereupon preſently a-ſhoare we went ,
and with our Dogs kill'd ſixe of them,after which,
the weather againe overcaſting , wee thought it to

C 3   little

little purpoſe to goe any further at that time , but reſolved to hunt all along the ſide of that hill, and ſo at night to returne unto our Tent. Going thus a-long, wee kill'd ſixe Deere more; which wee had no ſooner done, but it began to blow and raine, and to be very darke : whereupon wee haſted towards the Tent, there intending to refreſh our ſelves with vi-ctuals and with reſt for that night , and the next day to returne againe unto our hunting. This purpoſe of ours was by the foule weather the next day hin-dered : for it fell ſo blacke, ſo cold, and ſo windy, that we found it no way fitting for our purpoſe. La-ding therefore our owne Shallop with *Beares* and *Veniſon*; and another Shallop which we there found haled up , and left by the Ships Companie , as e-very yeare they uſe to doe : lading this other Shal-lop, I ſay, with the *Graves* of the *Whales* that had beene there boyled this preſent yeare, (which wee there found in heapes flung upon the ground) wee, dividing our ſelves into two equall companies, that is to ſay, *William Fakely* with one *Sea-man* and two *Land-men* with him, betaking themſelves unto one Shallop, and *Edward Pellham* with another *Sea-man* and two *Land-men* more with him, going into the other Shallop; wee all committed our ſelves unto the Sea, intending with the next faire weather to goe to *Bell Sownd* unto our Tent: which was the place wee ſet up our Reſt upon, to remaine at all the Winter.

Towards *Bell Sownd* therefore we went, with a purpoſe there to lay up our Store of what victuals wee had already gotten together; and with the next faire

faire winde to come hither againe, to trie if it were possible for us there to provide our selves of some more Venison for our Winter provision.

Having thus laden both our Shallops, appointed our Companie, and all ready now for our departure; wee were overtaken with the night, and there forced to stay upon the place. The next day was *Sunday*; wherefore wee thought it fit to sanctifie the *Rest* of it, and to stay our selves there untill *Munday*, and to make the best use we could of that good day, taking the best course wee could for the serying of God Almighty; although we had not so much as a Booke amongst us all, the whole time that wee staid in that Country.

The *Sabbath* day being shut up by the approaching night, we betooke our selves to our Rest: sleeping untill the Sunne awakened us by his beginning to shew himselfe upon the *Munday* morning. The day was no sooner peept, but up we got, fitting our selves and businesse for our departure. The weather was faire and cleere at the first; but after some foure houres rowing, the skie began so to overcast, and the winde to blow so hard, that we could not possibly get to *Bell Sownd* that night, but *Coved* halfe way, untill the next morning; at which time we recovered *Bottle Cove*. To which place when wee were once come, we found the winde (then at *Southwest*) to blow so hard, that it was impossible for us to reach *Bell Sownd*, but were forced to stay at *Bottle Cove* for that night. Our Shallops we made fast one unto another, with a Rope fastning the *head* of the one unto the *sterne* of the other; and so casting our

Grabnell

Grabnell or *Anchor* over-board, we left them riding in the *Cove*.

But fee now what a mifchance, for the tryall of our patience, and for the making of us to relye more upon his providence, than upon any outward meanes of our owne; God now fuffered to befall us: We being now all a-fhore, the *Southweft* winde blew fo hard and right into the *Cove*, that it made the Sea go *high*; our Anchor alfo *comming home* at the fame time, both our Shallops cafting alongft the fhoare, funke prefently in the Sea: wetting by this meanes our whole provifion, the weather with-all beating fome of it out of the Boates, which wee found fwimming up and downe the fhoare. For, comming out of our Tent in the meane time, judge you what a fight this was unto us, to fee by mif-chance, the beft part of our provifion (the onely hope of our lives) to be in danger utterly to be loft, (or at leaft fpoyled with the Sea-water,) for which we had taken fuch paines, and run fuch adventures in the getting. In this our miferie wee faw no way but one (and that a very defperate one) namely, to runne prefently into the *high-wrought* Sea, getting by that meanes into our Shallops to fave the re-mainder of our provifions, ready now to be wafht quite away by the billowes. A *Halfer* thereupon we got, which faftning unto our Shallops, wee, with a *Crabbe* or *Capftang*, by maine force of hand heaved them out of the water upon the fhoare. This done, all along the Sea fide we goe; feeking there and ta-king up fuch of our provifions, as were fwumme away from our Shallops. Having by this meanes gleaned

gleaned up all that could be gotten together, we resolved from thenceforth to let our Boates lye upon the shoare, till such time as the weather should prove faire and better; and then to goe over unto *Bell Sownd.*

The third of *September* the weather proving faire and good, we forthwith lanched our Shallops into the water, and in them wee that day got into *Bell Sownd.* Thither so soone as we were come, our first businesse was, to take our provision out of our Shallops into the Tent: our next, to take a particular view of the place, and of the great Tent especially; as being the place of our habitation for the ensuing Winter. This which we call the *Tent*, was a kinde of house (indeed) built of Timber and Boards very substantially, and covered with Flemish Tyles: by the men of which nation it had in the time of their trading thither, beene builded. Fourescore foot long it is, and in breadth fiftie. The use of it was for the *Coopers*, employed for the service of the *Company*, to worke, lodge, and live in, all the while they make caske for the putting up of the Trane Oyle. Our view being taken, we found the weather beginning to alter so strangely, and the nights and frosts so to grow upon us, that wee durst not adventure upon another hunting voyage unto *Green-harbour*, fearing the *Sownd* would be so frozen, that wee should never be able to get backe to our Tent againe. By land it was (we knew) in vaine for us to thinke of returning: for the land is so mountainous, that there is no travelling that way.

Things being at this passe with us, we bethought
D   our

our selves of building another smaller *Tent* with all
expedition : the place must of necessity be within
the greater Tent. With our best wits therefore taking a view of the place, we resolved upon the *South*
side. Taking downe another lesser Tent therefore,
(built for the *Land-men* hard by the other, wherein
in time of yeare they lay whilest they made their
Oyle) from thence we fetcht our materials. That
Tent furnisht us with 150 *Deale-boards*, besides
Posts or *Stancheons*, and *Rafters*. From three *Chimneys* of the *Furnaces* wherein they used to boyle
their *Oyles*, wee brought a thousand Bricks : there
also found wee three Hogsheads of very fine *Lyme*,
of which stuffe wee also fetcht another Hogshead
from *Battle Cove*, on the other side of the *Sownd*,
some three leagues distant. Mingling this Lyme
with the Sand of the Sea shore, we made very excel-
lent good morter for the laying of our Bricks : falling to worke whereupon, the weather was so ex-
treame cold, as that we were faine to make two fires
to keepe our morter from freezing. *William Fakely*
and my selfe undertaking the *Masonrie*, began to
raise a wall of one bricke thicknesse, against the inner planks of the side of the Tent. Whilest we were
laying of these Bricks, the rest of our Companie
were otherwise employed every one of them : some
in taking them downe, others in making of them
cleane, and in bringing them in baskets into the
Tent : Some in making morter, and hewing of
boards to build the other side withall : and two o-
thers all the while, in flaying of our Venison. And
thus having built the two outermost sides of the
                                                    Tent

Tent with Bricks and Morter, and our Bricks now
almost spent, wee were enforc't to build the other
two sides with Boards; and that in this manner.
First, we nayl'd our Deale boards on one side of the
Post or *Stancheon*, to the thicknesse of one foot;
and on the other side in like manner : and so filling
up the hollow place betweene with sand, it became
so tight and warme, as not the least breath of ayre
could possibly annoy us : Our Chimneys vent was
into the greater Tent; being the breadth of one
deale board, and foure foot long. The length of
this our Tent was twenty foot, and the breadth sixteene, the heighth tenne : our seeling being Deale
boards five or sixe times double, the middle of one,
joyning so close to the shut of the other, that no
winde could possibly get betweene. As for our
doore, besides our making it so close as possibly it
could shut, we lined it moreover with a bed that we
found lying there, which came over both the o-
pening and the shutting of it: As for windowes, we
made none at all : so that our light wee brought in
through the greater Tent, by removing two or three
tyles in the eaves, which light came to us through
the vent of our Chimney. Our next worke was, to
set up foure Cabbins, billetting our selves two
and two in a Cabbine. Our beds were the Deeres
skinnes dryed, which wee found to be extraordi-
nary warme, and a very comfortable kinde of lod-
ging to us in our distresse. Our next care then was
for firing to dresse our meate withall, and for keep-
ing away the cold Examining therefore all the
Shallops that had beene left a-shoare there by the
　　　　　Ships,

Ships, we found seven of them very crazie, and not serviceable for the next yeare. Those wee made bold withall, brake them vp, and carried them into our house, *stowing* them over the beames in manner of a floore; intending also to *stow* the rest of our firing over them, so to make the outer *Tent* the warmer, and to keepe withall the snow from drying through the tyles into the Tent: which snow would otherwise have covered every thing, and have hindered us in comming at what wee wanted. When the weather was now growne cold, and the dayes short, (or rather no dayes at all) wee made bold to *stave* some emptie Caske that were there left the yeare before: to the quantitie of 100 Tunne at least. We also made use of some planks, and of two old Coolers (wherein they cool'd their Oyle) and of whatsoever might well bee spared, without damnifying of the voyage the next yeare. Thus having gotten together all the firing that wee could possibly make, except we would make spoyle of the *Shallops* and *Coolers* that were there, which might easily have overthrowne the next yeares voyage, to the great hinderance of the Worshipfull Companie, whose servants we being, were every way carefull of their profite. Comparing therefore the samll quantitie of our wood, together with the coldnesse of the weather, and the length of time that there wee were likely to abide; wee cast about to husband our stocke as thriftily as wee could, devising to trie a new conclusion: Our tryall was this. When wee rak't up our fire at night, with a good quantitie of ashes and of embers, wee put into the

middʼst

midd'ft of it a piece of Elmen wood: where after
it had laine fixteene houres, we at our opening of it
found great ftore of fire upon it; whereupon wee
made a common practice of it ever after. It never
went out in eight moneths together or thereabouts.

Having thus provided both our *houfe* and *firing;*
upon the twelfth of *September* a fmall quantity of
drift yce, came driving to and fro in the *Scwnd.*
Early in the morning therefore wee arofe, and looking every where abroad, we at laft efpyed two *Sea-
horfes* lying a-fleepe upon a piece of yce : prefently
thereupon taking up an old *Harping* Iron that there
lay in the Tent,& faftning a *Grapnell* Roape unto it,
out lanch't wee our Boate to row towards them.
Comming fomething neere them, wee perceived
them to be faft a-fleepe: which my felfe, then fteer-
ing the Boate, firft perceiving, fpake to the rowers
to hold ftill their Oares, for feare of awaking them
with the crafhing of the yce; and I, skulling the
Boate eafily along, came fo neere at length unto
them, that the Shallops even touch't one of them.
At which inftant *William Fakely* being ready with
his *Harping Iron,* heav'd it fo ftrongly into the *old
one,* that hee quite difturbed her of her reft : after
which fhee receiving five or fixe thrufts with our
lances, fell into a founder fleepe of death. Thus having difpatch't the *old one,* the *younger* being loath
to leave her damme, continued fwimming fo long
about our Boate, that with our lances wee kill'd her
alfo. Haling them both after this into the Boate, we
rowed a-fhoare, flayed our *Sea-horfes,* cut them
in pieces, to roaft and eate them. The nineteenth

of

of the same moneth we saw other *Sea-horses*, sleeping also in like manner upon severall pieces of yce: but the weather being cold, they desired not to sleepe so much as before; and therefore could wee kill but one of them: of which one being right glad, we returned againe into our Tent.

The nights at this time, and the cold weather increased so fast upon us, that wee were out of all hopes of getting any more foode before the next Spring: our onely hopes were, to kill a *Beare* now and then, that might by chance wander that way. The next day therefore taking an exacter survey of all our victuals, and finding our proportion too small by halfe, for our time and companie; wee agreed among our selves to come to *Allowance*, that is, to stint our selves to one reasonable meale a day, and to keepe *Wednesdayes* and *Fridayes* Fasting dayes; excepting from the * *Frittars* or *Graves* of the *Whale* (a very loathsome meate) of which we allowed our selves sufficient to suffice our present hunger: and at this dyet we continued some three moneths or thereabouts.

* These be the Scraps of the Fat of the Whale, which are flung away after the Oyle is gotten out of it.

Having by this time finished what ever we possibly could invent, for our preservations in that desolate desert; our clothes & shooes also were so worne and torne (all to pieces almost) that wee must of necessity invent some new device for their reparations. Of *Roape-yarne* therefore, we made us *thread*, & of *Whale-bones* needles to sew our clothes withall. The nights were wax't very long, and by the tenth of *October* the cold so violent, that the Sea was frozen over : which had beene enough to haue

daunted

daunted the moſt aſſured reſolutions. At which
time our buſineſſe being over, and nothing now to
exerciſe our mindes upon ; our heads began then to
be troubled with a thouſand ſorts of imaginations.
Then had wee leiſure (more than enough) to com-
plaine our ſelves of our preſent and moſt miſerable
conditions. Then had wee time to bewaile our
wives and children at home; and to imagine what
newes our unfortunate miſcarriages muſt needes be
unto them. Then thought wee of our parents alſo,
and what a cutting Coraſive it would be to them,to
heare of the untimely deaths of their children. O-
therwhiles againe, wee revive our ſelves with ſome
comfort, that our friends might take,in hoping that
it might pleaſe *God* to preſerve us(even in this poore
eſtate)untill the next yeare.Sometimes did we varie
our griefes; complaining one while of the cruelty
of our *Maſter*, that would offer to leave us to theſe
diſtreſſes : and then preſently againe fell wee, not
onely to excuſe him , but to lament both him and
his companie, fearing they had beene overtaken
by the yce, and miſerably that way periſhed.

Thus tormented in mind with our doubts, our
feares, and our griefes; and in our bodies with hunger, cold, and wants ; that hideous monſter of de-
ſperation , began now to preſent his uglieſt ſhape
unto us : he now purſued us, hee now laboured to
ſeize upon us. Thus finding our ſelves in a *Laby-
rinth*,as it were,of a perpetuall miſerie,wee thought
it not beſt to give too much way unto our griefes;
fearing , they alſo would moſt of all have wrought
upon our weakeneſſe. Our prayers we now redou-
bled

bled unto the *Almighty*, for strength and patience, in these our miseries : and the *Lord* gracioufly liftned unto us, and granted thefe our petitions. By *his* affiftance therefore, wee fhooke off thefe thoughts, and cheer'd up our felves againe, to ufe the beft meanes for our prefervations.

Now therefore began we to thinke upon our *Venifon*, and the preferving of that; and how to order our *firing* in this cold weather. For feare therefore our *firing* fhould faile us at the end of the yeare, we thought beft to roaft every day halfe a *Deere*, and to *ftow* it in hogfheads. Which wee putting now in practice, wee forthwith filled three Hogfheads and an halfe; leaving fo much raw, as would ferve to roaft every Sabbath day a quarter : and fo for *Chriftmas* day, and the like.

This conclufion being made amongft us; then fell wee againe to bethinke us of our miferies, both paffed and to come : and how, (though if it pleafed God to give us life, yet fhould) we live as banifhed men, not onely from our friends, but from all other companie. Then thought we of the pinching cold, and of the pining hunger : thefe were our thoughts, this our difcourfe to paffe away the time withall. But as if all this miferie had beene too little, we prefently found another increafe of it : For, examining our provifions once more, wee found that all our *Frittars* of the *Whale* were almoft fpoyled with the wet that they had taken : after which by lying fo clofe together, they were now growne mouldie: And our *Beare* and *Venifon* we perceived againe not to amount to fuch a quantity, as to allow us five

meales

meales a weeke : whereupon we were faine to shor-
ten our stomacks of one meale more : so that for
the space of three moneths after that, we for foure
dayes in the weeke fed upon the unsavory and
mouldie *Frittars*, and the other three, we feasted it
with *Beare* and *Venison*. But as if it were not enough
for us to want meate, we now began to want light
also : all our meales proved suppers now ; for little
light could we see ; even the glorious Sunne (as if
unwilling to behold our miseries) masking his love-
ly face from us, under the sable vaile of cole-blacke
night. Thus from the fourteenth of *October*, till the
third of *February*, we never saw the *Sunne* ; nor did
hee all that time, ever so much as peepe above the
Horizon. But the *Moone* we saw at all times, day and
night (when the cloudes obscured her not) shining
as bright as shee doth in *England*. The Skie, 'tis
true, is very much troubled with thicke and blacke
weather all the Winter time : so that then, we could
not see the *Moone*, nor could discerne what point of
the Compasse shee bore upon us. A kinde of day-
light wee had indeed, which glimmer'd some eight
houres a day unto us, in *October* time I meane : for
from thence unto the first of *December*, even that
light was shortened tenne or twelve *minuts* a day
constantly : so that from the first of *December* till
the twentieth, there appeared no light at all; but all
was one continued night. All that wee could perceive was, that in a cleare season now and then, there
appeared a little glare of white, like some show of
day towards the *South* : but no light at all. And
this continued till the first of *Ianuary*, by which
E   time

time wee might perceive the day a little to increase. All this darkesome time, no certainety could wee have when it should be day, or when night: onely my selfe out of mine owne little judgement, kept the observation of it thus. First bearing in minde the number of the *Epact*, I made my addition by a day supposed, (though not absolutely to be known, by reason of the darkenesse) by which I judged of the age of the *Moone*: and this gave me my rule of the passing of the time; so that at the comming of the Ships into the *Port*, I told them the very day of the moneth, as directly as they themselves could tell mee.

At the beginning of this darkesome, irkesome time, wee sought some meanes of preserving light amongst us: finding therefore a piece of *Sheete-lead* over a seame of one of the Coolers; that we ript off, and made three Lampes of it: which maintaining with *Oyle* that wee found in the Coopers Tent, and *Roape-yarne* serving us in steed of Candle-weekes, wee kept them continually burning. And this was a great comfort to us in our extremity. Thus did we our best to preserve our selves; but all this could not secure us: for wee in our owne thoughts, accounted our selves but dead men, and that our Tent was then our darkesome dungeon, and we did but waite our day of tryall by our judge, to know whether wee should live or dye. Our extremities being so many, made us sometimes in impatient speeches to breake forth against the causers of our miseries: but then againe, our consciences telling us of our owne evill deservings; we tooke it either for a pu-

ntshment

nishment upon us for our former wicked lives ; or else for an example of Gods mercie, in our wonderfull deliverance. Humbling our selves therefore under the mighty hand of *God*, wee cast downe our selves before him in prayer, two or three times a day, which course we conftantly held all the time of our mifery.

The new yeare now begun, *as the dayes began to lengthen, fo the cold began to ftrengthen* : which cold came at laft to that extremitie, as that it would raife blifters in our flefh, as if wee had beene burnt with fire : and if wee touch't *iron* at any time, it would fticke to our fingers like *Bird-lime*. Sometimes if we went but out a-doores to fetch in a little water, the cold would nip us in fuch fort, that it made us as fore as if wee had beene beaten in fome cruell manner. All the firft part of the Winter, we found water under the yce, that lay upon the *Bache* on the Sea-fhoare. Which water iffued out of an high *Bay* or *Cliffe* of yce, and ranne into the hollow of the *Bache*, there remaining with a thicke yce over it: which yce, wee at one certaine place daily digging through with pick-axes, tooke fo much water as ferved for our drinking.

This continued with us untill the tenth of *Ianuarie* : and then were wee faine to make fhift with fnow-water; which we melted by putting hot Irons into it. And this was our drinke untill the twentieth of *May* following.

By the laft of *Ianuarie*, were the dayes growne to fome feven or eight houres long; and then we again tooke another view of our victuals : which we now found to grow so short, that it could no wayes last us above sixe weekes longer. And this bred a further feare of famine amongst us. But our recourse was in this, as in other our extremities, unto *Almighty God*; who had helps, we knew, though wee saw no hopes. And thus spent wee our time untill the third of *Februarie*. This proved a marvellous cold day; yet a faire and cleare one: about the middle whereof, all cloudes now quite dispersed, and nights sable curtaine drawne; *Aurora* with her golden face smiled once againe upon us, at her rising out of her bed: for now the glorious Sunne with his glittering beames, began to guild the highest tops of the loftie mountaines. The brightnesse of the Sunne, and the whitenesse of the snow, both together was such, as that it was able to have revived even a dying spirit. But to make a new addition to our new joy, we might perceive two Beares, (a shee one with her Cubbe) now comming towards our Tent: whereupon wee straight arming our selves with our lances, issued out of the Tent to await her comming. Shee soone cast her greedy eyes upon us; and with full hope of devouring us, shee made the more haste unto us: but with our hearty lances we gave her such a welcome, as that shee fell downe upon the ground, tumbling up and downe, and biting the very snow for anger. Her Cubbe seeing this, by flight escaped us. The weather now was so cold, that longer wee were not able to stay abroad: retiring therefore into our Tent, wee first warmed our selves; and then out againe to draw the dead Beare in unto us. Wee flaied her, cut her into pieces

of

of a *Stone* weight or thereabouts, which ferv'd us for our dinners. And upon this Beare we fed fome twenty dayes; for fhee was very good flefh,and better than our Venifon. This onely mifchance wee had with her: that upon the eating of her Liver, our very skinnes peeled off: for mine owne part, I being ficke before, by eating of that Liver, though I loft my skinne, yet recovered I my health upon it. Shee being fpent, either wee muft feeke fome other meate, or elfe fall aboard with our roaft Venifon in the Caske, which we were very loath to doe for feare of famifhing, if fo be *that* fhould be thus fpent, before the Fleete came out of *England.* Amid'ft thefe our feares,it pleafed God to fend divers *Beares* unto our Tent; fome fortie at leaft, as we accounted. Of which number we kill'd feven: That is to fay, the fecond of *March* one ; the fourth, another ; and the tenth, a wonderfull great *Beare* ,fixe foote high at leaft. All which we flayed and roafted upon woodden fpits,(having no better kitchen-furniture than that, and a frying-pan, which we found in the Tent.) They were as good favory meate, as any beefe could be. Having thus gotten good ftore of fuch foode, wee kept not our felves now to fuch ftraight allowance as before ; but eate frequently two or three meales a-day : which began to increafe ftrength and abilitie of body in us.

By this, the cheerfull dayes fo faft increafed, that the feverall forts of *Fowles,* which had all the Winter-time avoyded thofe quarters, began now againe to reforthither, unto their Summer-abiding. The fixteenth of *March,* one of our two *Maftive Dogges*

E 3   went

went out of the Tent from us in the morning : but
from that day to this he never more returned to us,
nor could wee ever heare what was become of him.
The *Fowles* that I before spake of, conſtantly uſe
every *Spring* time to reſort unto that Coaſt, being
uſed to breede there moſt abundantly. Their foode
is a certaine kinde of ſmall fiſhes. Yearely upon
the abundant comming of theſe *Fowles*, the *Foxes*
which had all this Winter kept their Burrowes under the Rockes, began now to come abroad, and
ſeeke for their livings. For them wee ſet up three
Trappes like Rat-trappes, and bayted them with the
ſkinnes of theſe *Fowles*, which wee had found upon
the ſnow; they falling there in their flight from the
hill whereupon they bred, towards the Sea. For
this *Fowle*, being about the bigneſſe of a *Ducke*, hath
her legs placed ſo cloſe unto her rumpe, as that
when they alight once upon the land, they are very
hardly (if ever) able to get up againe, by reaſon of
the miſplacing of their legs, and the weight of their
bodies; but being in the water, they raiſe themſelves
with their pinions well enough. After wee had
made Theſe Trappes, and ſet them apart one from
another in the ſnow, we caught fiftie *Foxes* in them:
all which wee roaſted, and found very good meate
of them. Then tooke we a Beares ſkinne, and laying the fleſh ſide upward, wee made Springes of
Whales bone, wherewith wee caught about 60. of
thoſe *Fowles*, about the bigneſſe of a pigeon.

Thus continued wee untill the firſt of *May*; and
the weather then growing warme; wee were now
pretty able to goe abroad to ſeeke for more proviſi-
on

fion. Every day therefore abroad we went; but nothing could we encounter withall, untill the 24. of *May*; when efpying a *Bucke*, wee thought to have kill'd him with our Dogge: but he was growne fo fat and lazie, that hee could not pull downe the Deere. Seeking further out therefore, we found abundance of *Willocks* egges; (which is a *Fowle* about the bigneffe of a *Ducke*) of which egges though there were great ftore, yet wee being but two of us together, brought but thirty of them to the Tent that day; thinking the next day to fetch a thoufand more of them: but the day proved fo cold, with fo much *Eafterly* winde, that wee could not ftirre out of our Tent.

Staying at home therefore upon the 25. of *May*, we for that day omitted our ordinary cuftome. Our order of late (fince the faire weather) was, every day, or every fecond day, to goe up to the top of a mountaine, to fpie if wee could difcerne the water in the Sea; which untill the day before we had not feene. At which time, a ftorme of winde comming out of the Sea, brake the maine yce within the *Sownd*: after vvhich, the vvinde comming *Eafterly*, carried all the yce into the Sea, and cleared the *Sownd* a great vvay, although not neere the fhoare at firft, feeing the cleare vvater came not neere out Tent by three miles at leaft.

This 25. of *May* therefore, vvee all day ftaying in the Tent, there came two Ships of *Hull* into the *Sownd*: vvho knowing that there had been men left there the yeare before; the *Mafter* (full of defire to know vvhether vve vvere alive or dead) man'd out a
Shallop

Shallop from the Ship; with order to row as farre up the *Sownd* as they could, and then to hale up their Shallop , and travell over-land upon the snow unto the Tent. These men at their comming a-shore, found the Shallop which we had haled from our Tent into the water, with a purpose to goe seeke some Sea-horses the next faire weather: the Shallop being then already fitted with all necessaries for that enterprize. This sight brought them into a quandary; and though this encounter made them hope, yet their admiration made them doubt , that it was not possible for us still to remaine alive. Taking therefore our lances out of the Boate , towards the Tent they come ; wee never so much as perceiving of them : for wee were all gathered together , now about to goe to prayers in the inner Tent; onely *Thomas Ayers* was not yet come in to us out of the greater Tent. The *Hull* men now comming neere our Tent, haled it with the usuall word of the Sea crying *Hey*, he answered againe with *Ho*; which sudden answer almost amazed them all, causing them to stand still, halfe afraid at the matter. But we within hearing of them, joyfully came out of the Tent; all blacke as we were with the smoake, and with our clothes all tattered with wearing. This uncouth sight made them further amazed at us : but perceiving us to be the very men left there all the yeare; with joyfull hearts embracing us , and wee them a-gaine, they came with us into our Tent. Comming thus in to us , wee shewed them the courtesie of the house, and gave them such victuals as we had; which was Venison roasted foure moneths before , and a

Cuppe

Cuppe of cold water; which for noveltie sake they kindly accepted of us.

Then fell wee to aske them what *newes* . and of the state of the Land at home ? and when the *London* Fleete would come ? to all which, they returned us the best answers they could. Agreeing then to leave the Tent; with them wee went to their Shallop, and so a-board the Ship; where we were welcomed after the heartiest and kindest *English* manner; and there we stayed our selves untill the comming of the *London* Fleete, which we much longed for : hoping by them to heare from our friends in *England.* Wee were told that they would be there the next day; but it was full three dayes ere they came, which seemed to us as tedious a three dayes, as any we had yet endured: so mnch we now desired to heare from our friends, our wives and children.

The 28. of *May,* the *London* Fleete came into the *Port* to our great comfort. A-board the *Admirall* we went, unto the right noble Captaine, *Captaine William Goodler,* who is worthy to be honoured by all Sea-men for his courtesie and bounty. This is the Gentleman that is every yeare chiefe Commander of this Fleete; and right worthy he is so to be, being a very wise man, and an expert Mariner as most be in *England,* none dispraised. Unto this Gentleman right welcome we were; and joyfully by him received : hee giving order, that we should have any thing that was in the Ship, that might doe us good, and increase our strength; of his owne charges giving us apparell also, to the value of twenty pounds worth.

F   Thus

Thus after fourteene dayes of refreshment, wee grew perfectly well all of us : whereupon the noble Captaine sent *William Fakely*, and *Iohn Wyse*, (*Masons* own Apprentice)and *Thomas Ayers* the Whale-Cutter,with *Robert Good fellow*, unto Master *Masons* Ship, according as themselves desired. But thinking there to be as kindly welcomed,as the lost *Prodigall*; these poore men after their enduring of so much misery, which through his meanes partly they had undergone: no sooner came they a-board his ship, but he most unkindly call'd them *Run-awayes*, with other harsh and unchristian termes, farre enough from the civility of an honest man. Noble Captaine *Goodler* understanding all these passages, was right sorie for them, resolving to send for them againe, but that the weather proved so bad and uncertaine. I for mine owne part, remained with the Captaine still at *Bottle Cove*, according to mine owne desire : as for the rest of us that staid with him, hee preferr'd the *Land-men* to row in the Shallops for the killing of the *Whales* ; freeing them thereby from their toylesome labour a-shoare ; bettering their *Meanes* besides. And all these favours did this worthy *Gentleman* for us.

Thus were wee well contented now to stay there till the twentieth of *August*; hoping then to returne into our native Countrey : which day of departure being come, and we imbarked, with joyfull hearts we set sayle through the foaming *Ocean*, and though cross'd sometimes with contrary windes homeward bound ; yet our proper ships at last came safely to an Anchor in the River of *Thames* : to our great joy
and

and comfort, and the Merchants benefite. And thus by the bleffing of *God* came wee all eight of us well home, fafe and found: where the Worfhipfull Companie our Mafters, the *Mufcovie* Merchants, have fince dealt wonderfully well by us. For all which moft mercifull Prefervation, and moft wonderfully powerfull Deliverance, all honour, praife, and glory by unto the great God, the fole Author of it. He grant us to make the right ufe of it, *Amen.*

FINIS.